Insider's Guide to Estes Park and Rocky Mountain National Park

Updated for 2024

Josh and Emma Adams

Estes Park
INSIDER

Estes Park Insider LLC

Second edition: February 2024
ISBN: 979-8-87-927799-9

The authors worked diligently to ensure the information in this book was correct at
the time of publication. However, the authors do not assume any liability for loss or
damage caused by errors or omissions.

The recommendations included in this book are based on the authors' actual
experiences and they have tried to represent everything as faithfully as possible.

Dedication

This guide is dedicated to the
millions of devoted visitors to
Estes Park and Rocky Mountain
National Park.

Contents

Chapter 1

Introduction

We rolled out the first edition of this guide in 2023 to help you have the best time possible in Estes Park and Rocky Mountain National Park. This newly updated version has that same goal.

Generally speaking, there aren't many things that change much from year to year in small mountain towns. However, this year was a little different.

First, the National Park Service updated some of the details associated with the timed entry permits. Learn more in the **RMNP Timed Entry Reservations** chapter.

Second, a few major construction projects are still in progress, including **The Loop**, which completely changes the downtown traffic pattern. You'll either be amazed or befuddled, but you'll definitely want to better understand the new pattern before you get stuck in the middle of it. You can learn more about our construction projects in a new chapter titled, "**The Loop – Downtown Reconfigured**."

Finally, after another year of dining, shopping, and living in Estes Park, we've updated our reviews and recommendations for dining, activities, and Must-See Destinations.

Just like the previous edition, we provide answers, strategies and suggestions for the most commonly asked questions, including:

- The best places to see wildlife.

- How to win the Timed Entry Reservation game.

- Getting in the park without a Timed Entry Reservation.

- Alternative routes (and strategies) to avoid traffic jams and bottlenecks.

- Some of the best dining options.

- Easy hikes and fun things to do with the family.

- Lots of money-saving and time-saving tips.

Why you can trust our advice.

#1 We came to Estes Park for our family vacations (and a few romantic getaways) for more than 25 years. We learned a lot over the years, so we think we have a really good understanding of your desires and expectations. Now that we're year-round locals, we've learned even more things that can help you maximize your vacation enjoyment.

#2 We don't work for the town's tourism machine. We don't accept advertising. You're getting honest, straightforward advice and recommendations from people who are a lot like you.

#3 Best of all, we won't waste your time. We get to the point ... *fast*. No marketing. No PR. No fluff.

One more thing...

Keep your eyes peeled for the "Highly Recommended" notations in this guide. These are more commonly found in the chapter titled, "Eating In Estes Park" recommendations, but there are a few sprinkled in other places, too.

♥ Highly Recommended

Okay! Let's get started!

Chapter 2

Getting Around in Estes Park

Strategies to Help You Navigate the Crowds

Every year, around 4.5 million people come to explore and enjoy Rocky Mountain National Park. And most of you come right through Estes Park on your way.

4,500,000 Visitors Per Year

Even a large city would be challenged to have that many people funneling into and through their downtown area. Estes Park has fewer options to redirect all of that flow, but we've come up with a few strategies that can help you avoid or successfully navigate the crowds and logjams. That's what this chapter is about.

There's one really major change this year that you need to know about – **The Loop**.

The Town of Estes Park – along with federal and state experts and consultants – have been working on a plan that should be completed in late 2024. This project is dubbed, "The Loop," and is designed to minimize gridlock and delays without reducing access to the downtown shops and restaurants.

There's been much debate as to whether it will work or not. But, ready or not, we'll soon find out.

At the time we updated and republished this book, construction crews were still on the scene doing some of the finishing work. However, the new traffic patterns are locked in place.

To ensure you clearly understand how the downtown traffic pattern has changed, please refer to the new chapter, "**The Loop – Downtown Reconfigured.**"

Even if the end goal of "The Loop" is realized, it's certainly not a cure-all. Challenges with traffic will always remain. So, we still encourage you to review the following strategies so you can spend more time enjoying Estes Park and RMNP instead of wasting your family time sitting in gridlock.

Understanding Traffic Flow

Most of the vehicles destined for RMNP arrive from the east. These cars and trucks (and motorcycles and buses and campers) must drive into Estes Park on one of three different roads. Most of that traffic eventually feeds right into the heart of downtown and then exits downtown on the way to the Beaver Meadows or the Fall River entrance gates for RMNP.

Three roads in. Two roads out. And, they intersect in the middle of downtown.

Downtown is the biggest choke
point.

Even with The Loop Project in place, we still believe the best way to avoid all that traffic is to avoid going through downtown as much as you can.

We're not saying to avoid going downtown. To the contrary, downtown has a lot of great shops, restaurants, and more. We're just saying to avoid going through downtown if your actual destination is RMNP.

There aren't many choices here, but every minute helps. So here are three options that can help you avoid some of the log jams.

Options to Consider

- Before you leave home or your hotel room, condo, cabin, or campsite, access your favorite mapping/traffic application (e.g., Google Maps, Apple Maps, Waze, etc.) to see where the largest backups exist. There are also several webcams you can use to gauge traffic. (See "Mobile Apps and Websites.")

- If you want to enter RMNP via the Fall River entrance gate, consider taking West Wonderview Ave. (Highway 34). This is the road that passes in front of the Stanley Hotel. Taking this bypass will usually save you considerable time when compared to driving through downtown.

- If you're targeting the Beaver Meadows entrance for RMNP (Highway 36), consider bypassing downtown by using Highway 7 (S. St. Vrain Ave) and Mary's Lake Road instead. You'll first need to connect with Highway 7 on the southeast side of town and then head south a few miles to reach Mary's Lake Road. Turn west on Mary's Lake Road and you'll eventually connect to Highway 36 just east of the Beaver Meadows entrance gate. (This is the intersection adjacent to the *Country Market*.) Take a left and you're on your way ... assuming traffic at the gate hasn't backed up that far.

Reminder: Wherever you're coming from, if you need to arrive at RMNP at a certain time (based on your Timed Entry Reservation), do yourself a favor and allow for extra time to get through town on the way to your intended gate. However, keep in mind that there can still be long lines (very long lines) at the entrance gates. The mapping apps and webcams mentioned earlier are key to helping you plan how much extra time you may need.

Seasons and Scenery (and traffic overload)

In the off-season (Nov thru April), it's generally very easy to get around town and into RMNP. That all starts to change in May when the weekend visitor count starts growing.

Traffic steadily increases through the summer months until September, which is when we reach (and exceed) maximum capacity just about every day of the week.

Options to Consider

Avoid visiting during the peak season (June to October). We know ... this is tough. After all, it's summer! You want to get outside and hike or drive through the spectacular scenery in our beautiful weather. Or it's the fall and you want to watch the big bull elk fight for their mates with the background of fall foliage. Both are valid points for coming here during peak seasons, but you'll just have to be okay with dealing with a lot more people and cars.

Before we relocated here, our family had some of our best and most memorable times in Estes Park during the off-season. Christmas, Thanksgiving, and Easter in Estes Park are all outstanding.

It's way less busy. Traffic is easy. Parking is wide open (and free). Lodging is less expensive and more available. Most shops and restaurants remain open but without the long waiting lines. And the animals seem to be more concentrated around town.

If that's not enough, you should know that winter is absolutely stunning in Estes Park. The surrounding mountains are all topped with snow. And the seasonal lighting downtown and around the River Walk is outstanding.

Frankly, it's a completely different experience, and certainly worth trying. Just bring your snow boots, hats and puff jackets.

If you do want to enjoy Estes Park in the peak season, consider arriving on a Monday or Tuesday and then leaving on Friday morning. Midweek trips can save you a lot of time and headaches.

There will still be a lot of people, but not nearly as many as those who come on the weekends.

Accommodation Selection

Everyone has their criteria when choosing a particular place to bed down at night. Here's one more to consider.

Staying at accommodations west of downtown will help you avoid a lot of the downtown traffic issues.

Options to Consider

- Immediately before the Fall River entrance to RMNP on Highway 34, you'll find an abundance of hotels, inns, chalets, cabins, and condos that are available for rent.

- Highway 66 splits off Highway 36 just before you get to the Beaver Meadow Entrance. Take this road and you'll find a multitude of options, including the area's largest RV resort/campground, cabins, condos, short-term rentals, VRBOs, and the YMCA of the Rockies.

- Finally, if you want an option that puts you right in the heart of RMNP, consider camping inside the park. In addition to avoiding traffic, you also won't need to buy a Timed Entry Reservation. (See "RMNP Camping Options")

Time of Day

Yes, we understand. You're on vacation. You want to sleep in. Guess what? So does everyone else. You can use this to your advantage.

Get Up and Get Out Early (Earlier)

Here are five really good reasons to do this.

- There is way less traffic.

- The lines are shorter. Entrance gates, restaurants, grocery store checkouts, gas pumps, etc. Just about every line you could be in will be shorter.

- There are more parking spaces open. (In RMNP *and* in town.)

- There are many more animals out and about in RMNP in the early morning (and at dusk).

- If you're a photographer, you likely already know about the "golden hour" right after sunrise and right before sunset.

Shift Your Daily Routine

If you can, consider shifting your normal daily schedule one or two hours ahead.

If you're dining out, eat lunch at 11 am instead of noon - when everybody else will be in line ahead of you. It works even better for dinner.

If you came here from the Eastern or Central time zones, your body clock is already an hour or two ahead of Colorado's Mountain time zone. Stick with your home-based patterns! Just go to bed at your normal "home" time and then wake up at your normal "home" time.

Alternatives to Driving Yourself

The convenience of having your own car close by is always enjoyable, but there are ways to get around without one.

In-town Shuttles

The Town of Estes Park understands the problems associated with all that traffic downtown and its dire lack of parking spots. So, a few years ago, they instituted a free shuttle service for visitors and locals alike.

These shuttles will not get you into RMNP, but they do offer a great way to get you where you're going in and around Estes Park.

There are five routes in total, with each route being identified by a different color. All start at the Estes Park Visitor Center, branch off in different directions, and then return to the visitor center.

- **Red** - Downtown

- **Yellow** – West on Highway 34, past the Stanley Hotel to the Rocky Mountain Gateway

- **Silver** – Along Highway 7 to the Estes Park Events Center and the Estes Park Community Center

- **Brown** – West on Highway 36 and Riverside Drive out to the YMCA of the Rockies

- **Blue** – East on Highway 34 to Dry Gulch Road

These shuttles run from Memorial Day weekend through mid-October.

A more detailed schedule can be obtained at the Estes Park Visitor Center.

RMNP Shuttles

If your goal is to get into RMNP, the Hiker Shuttle can take you from the Estes Park Visitor Center to the Park-and-Ride Transit Hub on Bear Lake Road. Once there, you can jump on one of their in-park shuttles to travel to the various stops and trailheads on Bear Lake Road and throughout Moraine Park. Note: Shuttle Reservations are required.

More info about these shuttles can be found in the "RMNP's Hiker Shuttle Service" section found in the "Accessing RMNP Without a Timed Entry Reservation" chapter.

Rideshares (Lyft, Uber)

Rideshare services are available in Estes Park. However, the number of drivers is more limited than in larger cities, especially during the off-season. Our best advice is to check your app before committing to this as your primary form of transportation.

Chapter 3

The Loop – Downtown Reconfigured

Fingers Crossed!

The Downtown Estes Park Loop, aka, "The Loop," is a $42 million project that's intended to ease traffic congestion in Estes Park town while speeding visitors to and from Rocky Mountain National Park.

> Key downtown roads have been converted into a one-way loop.

Simply stated, by converting portions of the primary downtown roads into a one-way loop, traffic should be able to move more freely while still enabling visitor access to parking and additional side streets.

The new traffic pattern changed in December 2023, so some of you may have already given it a test drive. However, construction is not slated to be finished until winter 2024.

Ready or not, The Loop awaits. Please review the map below to familiarize yourself with the new pattern.

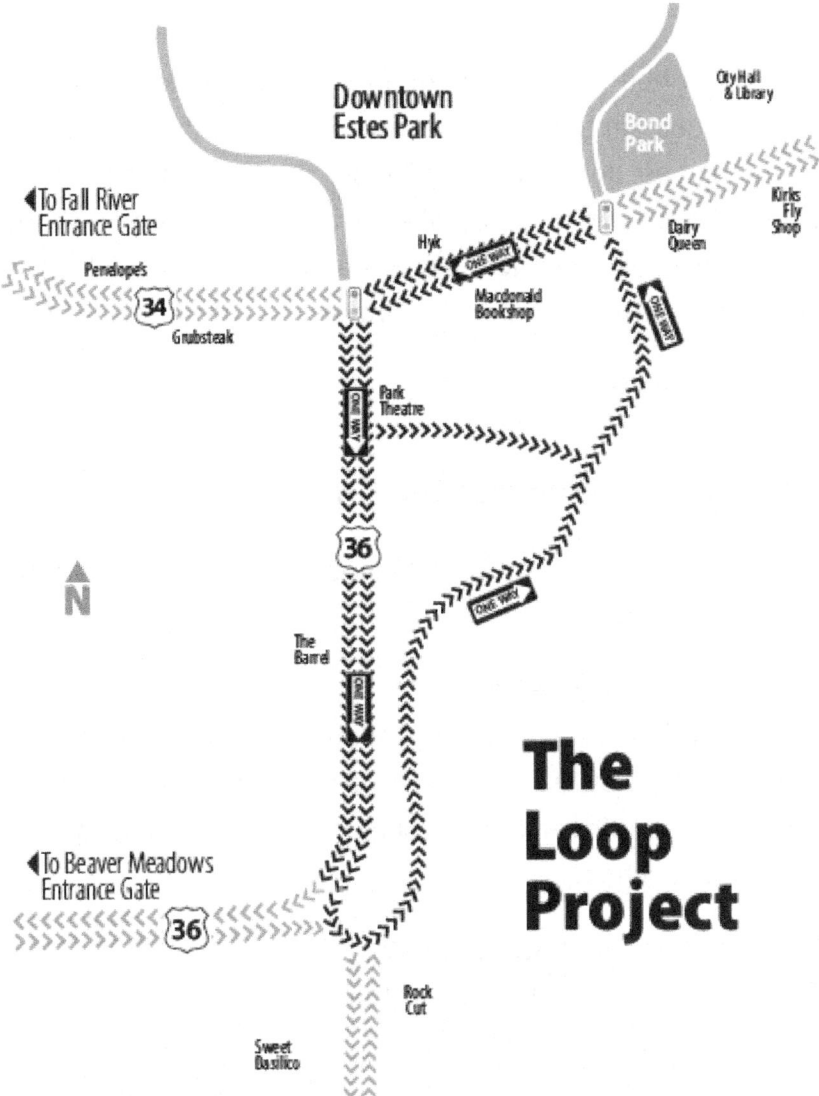

Downtown
Estes Park

Bond
Park

City Hall
& Library

To Fall River
Entrance Gate

Kirks
Fly
Shop

Hyk

Penelope's

Dairy
Queen

ONE WAY

34

Macdonald
Bookshop

ONE WAY

Grubsteak

N

Park
Theatre

ONE WAY

36

ONE WAY

The
Barrel

ONE WAY

The
Loop
Project

To Beaver Meadows
Entrance Gate

36

Rock
Cut

Sweet
Basilico

The project was designed and funded by the Federal Highway Administration, the Colorado Department of Transportation (CDOT), and the Town of Estes Park. Though it's been in the making for several years, local support has been hotly divided from the very start.

Some of our citizens were strongly opposed to the use of eminent domain to obtain property (including the place that made the best donuts in town!). More than a few business owners have been unhappy when access to their stores/shops was reduced by construction crews and equipment. And, many don't believe that traffic will improve.

Only time will tell.

Other Traffic/Construction Changes

We also have a couple other traffic and construction projects that may be of interest to you.

New Traffic Circle on Highway 36
A new traffic circle has been installed at the intersection of Highway 36 (N. St. Vrain Ave) and Community Drive. This is just south of Lake Estes and was designed to help eliminate gridlock at the intersection.

Fall River Entrance Gate to RMNP
The National Park Service is most of the way through the construction of an entirely new entrance at Fall River. This project features three new gates (including one fast-pass gate), a new entrance sign, newly paved roads, and a modern utility stack so the Rangers can work safer, faster, better, and more efficiently.

Having three entrance gates instead of two should also help minimize the backup that often occurs during peak season.

To learn more, see:
https://www.nps.gov/romo/planyourvisit/fall-river-entrance-construction-project.htm

Moraine Park Campground

Major changes are underway as RMNP completes the Moraine Park Campground and Utility Restoration Project. This is primarily an infrastructure project to improve the water, wastewater, and electrical systems for the campground itself as well as other facilities on the east side of the park.

The campground was closed in May 2023 once work got underway, but it should reopen this summer (fingers crossed).

To learn more see:
https://www.nps.gov/romo/getinvolved/moraine-park-campground-and-headquarters-east-utility-rehabilitation-project.htm

Chapter 4

Parking

Good Luck!

At peak season, and during most special events, finding a parking place is – at best – a challenge (understatement).

Free Parking

The Visitor Center

The first parking option at the Visitor Center is an outdoor lot on Big Thompson Road (Highway 34). The second option is a covered parking garage located behind the Visitor Center and across the river. The four-story Visitor Center Parking Garage holds 415 cars. However, to get your vehicle in one of those spots, you'll need to get on Highway 36/Highway 7 first. You can park for free in both of these lots all day.

(Note: RVs, buses, and trailers are not allowed in the parking garage.)

From either of these options, it's a fairly short walk to downtown. If you don't want to walk, you can take the Red Estes Park Town Shuttle into downtown and back again.

Estes Park Event Center Parking

The Estes Park Events Center (1125 Rooftop Way) offers a large parking area for visitors, including spaces for 20 RVs. From here, you can jump on the Silver Line of the Estes Shuttle to get to the Visitor Center.

On-street Parking

There's a very limited supply of free, on-street parking in the downtown area. However, most of these spots have a one-hour or three-hour time limit.

Paid Parking

Assuming you can find an open spot, you'll need to pay for the privilege of parking in most of the downtown parking lots. The parking lot east of City Hall and the Library is the largest.

From Memorial Day to mid-October and between 10 am to 5 pm MT, parking in these lots costs $2 per hour. For the rest of the year, parking there is free.

You can pay for your parking at the kiosks in the parking lot, or by using the ParkMobile app, which is available on the Apple App Store or from Google Play.

You can find a downloadable parking map on the Town of Estes Park Website.

Parking Enforcement

Parking in the paid lots is rigorously monitored and enforced by a parking patrol. In 2023, this process was carried out by a harmless-looking white compact car equipped with cameras and computers. It drives through the rows of cars while simultaneously taking pictures of the license plates. When your license plate is compared to the data entered in the kiosk or via the mobile app, they know if your parking time has expired. If it has, you're issued a ticket.

While that seems a little cold (though extremely efficient), it does provide one benefit for us all. As the Parking Patrol rolls through each lot, it also counts the open slots and reports that back to another mobile app designed to help us all find open slots.

So, if you want to see what parking availability looks like downtown, download the "Estes Parking" mobile app from the Apple App Store or Google Play.

Chapter 5

RMNP Timed Entry Reservations

Unloved, but needed.

Generally speaking, people come to Estes Park to enjoy the scenery, animals, and calm (or challenges) associated with Rocky Mountain National Park. However, the Timed Entry Permit process has been creating a lot of issues and confusion for many. That's exactly why this chapter is devoted to it.

Overview

With 4.5 million visitors every year, overcrowding is nothing new to regular visitors of Rocky Mountain National Park. The park itself is huge – a whopping 415 square miles. However, the road system that provides access and parking to all of those visitors is tiny in comparison.

To avoid the incredible congestion and minimize the damage being done to park resources, the National Park Service implemented a Timed Entry Reservation process in 2020. The intent of this was to throttle and limit the number of vehicles allowed in the park, with hopes for shorter lines, more parking spots, increased safety, and freedom of motion.

Like it or not, it's here to stay. So, we all just need to deal with it as best we can. The best advice we can provide is to learn how it works so you can plan accordingly.

The keyword here is "plan."

(Note: The following info describes how the Timed Entry Reservation process works in 2024. This may change in the future, so check for updates.)

The Timed Entry Reservation process can be a little confusing, so let's break it down into smaller components.

***

Entry Permit vs Timed Entry Reservation

Entry Permit

Regardless of when you come to Rocky Mountain National Park, at least one person in your vehicle must have an entry permit. This could be a daily or weekly pass or another qualifying NPS park pass, such as the ***America the Beautiful National Park Pass*** or the ***Senior Pass***. With this entry pass, you can enter any of the primary gates, as well as Longs Peak, Lily Lake, Lumpy Ridge, East Inlet, and North Inlet.

The only exception to this is when the NPS hosts entrance fee-free days. In 2024, those days are:
- January 15 – Martin Luther King Jr. Day
- April 20 – First Day of National Park Week
- August 4 – Great American Outdoors Day
- September 28 – National Public Lands Day
- November 11 – Veterans Day

Timed Entry Reservation

Timed Entry Reservations are required *in addition* to the standard Entry Fees and Passes.

In 2024, a Timed Entry Reservation is required to enter Rocky Mountain National Park from **May 24 to October 27**.

Timed Entry Reservations are required: **May 24 to October 27, 2024**.

How to Purchase Your Timed Entry Reservation

Timed Entry Reservations can be purchased using one of the following five methods:
- Website: recreation.gov

- Recreation.gov mobile app
- Toll-free phone number: 877-444-6777
- Intl. Telephone: +1 606-515-6777
- TTD Telephone: 877-833-6777

Note: Timed Entry Reservations cannot be picked up at the entrance gates or within the RMNP Visitor Centers.

Reservations can be obtained far in advance (see "Advanced Schedule" below), or they can be purchased on a next-day basis on the day before entry is desired (see "Next-Day Passes" below).

Advanced Schedule

The advanced schedule option enables you to buy Timed Entry passes a full month ahead of the day(s) you think you'll want to go into RMNP.

To take advantage of this, you'll need to know your travel plans at least a month ahead of time.

This option favors the "planners" – not the impromptu travelers.

- On May 1, 2024, you can purchase reservations for any date from May 24 to June 30.

- On June 1, 2024, you can purchase reservations for any date in July.

- On July 1, 2024, you can purchase reservations for any date in August.

- On August 1, 2024, you can purchase reservations for any

date in September.

- On September 1, 2024, you can purchase reservations for any date from October 1-27.

These tickets go on sale at 8 am MT on the dates noted above. Even though you're planning your trip at least a month ahead of time, **you still need to be ready to reserve these tickets at 8 am MT**, especially when seeking entrance on the weekends. See the following section titled, "How to Maximize Your Chances of Getting a Timed Entry Reservation" for more info.

Up to 10 reservations can be purchased per session. If you want to purchase more than 10 reservations, you'll need to sign out of your recreation.gov account after booking your first 10 reservations, and then sign back in for up to 10 more.

Next-Day Passes

This is the only option for impromptu travelers to obtain Timed Entry passes.

Originally, only advanced schedule passes were available. Let's just say a lot of people were very unhappy about it. So, park officials decided to set aside a portion of the passes for next-day use.

In 2023, 40% of the available passes were reserved for next-day use.

Next-Day Passes Sell Out Fast.

Next-day passes go on sale at 7 pm MT on the day before entry is desired. So, if you want to get into RMNP on a Saturday for example, our advice is to be online and ready to go at 7 pm MT on Friday.

To be clear, for your best chance of obtaining a Next-Day Pass, **you'll need to be online at 7 pm – not 7:01 pm or 7:02 pm or 7:03 pm.** That's how fast these tickets can sell out.

See the following section titled, "How to Maximize Your Chances of Getting a Timed Entry Reservation" for more info.

Timed Entry Reservation Options

There are two types of Timed Entry Reservations and each of them costs $2, in addition to the entry fee. Let's break down the differences.

Park Access+ Pass

The **Park Access+** pass enables admission to the entire park, including the Bear Lake Road corridor.

Bear Lake Road is a two-lane road that runs from Beaver Meadows to Bear Lake. This section of the park contains many of the most desirable (and accessible) hot spots for visitors, including Moraine Park, Sprague Lake, and Bear Lake. It also contains numerous popular trailheads including Glacier Gorge, Emerald/Nymph/Dream Lakes, Bierstadt Lake, Fern Lake, Cub Lake, etc.

The more restrictive **Park Access+** pass is needed because:

- This is a very desirable part of RMNP for visitors.

- It's a relatively short, dead-end road. One way in; the same way out.

- Parking is limited.

Before Timed Entry Reservations were instituted, the traffic and gridlock on Bear Lake Road were unforgiving and immensely difficult to deal with. The experience is much more relaxed and enjoyable now.

Park Access+ passes are available for the following two-hour time increments:
- 5-7 am MT
- 6-8 am MT
- 8-10 am MT
- 10 am-12 pm MT
- 12-2 pm MT
- 2-4 pm MT
- 4-6 pm MT

Your vehicle must initially enter the Bear Lake Road corridor during the timeframe shown on your reservation.

You can stay in this part of the park as long as you like. If you enter at Bear Lake and then leave again, you can spend the rest of the day exploring other portions of Rocky Mountain National Park. However, you cannot return to the Bear Lake corridor until after 2 pm.

Park Access Pass (no "plus")

The **Park Access** pass enables access to everywhere in RMNP except for the Bear Lake Road corridor.

Park Access passes are available for the following two-hour time increments:
- 9-11 am MT
- 11 am-1 pm MT
- 12-2 pm MT

Don't Miss Your Time Slot

If you're late to the gate and you miss your two-hour time slot, your Timed Entry Reservation pass is no longer usable.

For example, if you purchased a **Park Access+** pass for the 6-8 am time slot on Bear Lake Road, and don't show up at the gate until 8:30 am, you will (usually) be asked to turn around and exit the corridor.

In the early days of the Timed Entry process, the rangers may have let us pass through if we were early or late by a few minutes. However, it seems like the time limits are being enforced a little more now. For example, we've been told to turn around and get back in line if we're too early, or (gasp) exit entirely if we're running late. So, do your best to get to the appropriate gate on time.

To ensure you make it to the actual gate by your assigned time, check your phone's mapping application to see how long the lines are at the entrance gates and plan accordingly. You can also take advantage of the webcams located at each entrance gate, which will show you how backed up they are at any given time of the day. See: https://www.nps.gov/romo/learn/photosmultimedia/webcams.htm

How to Maximize Your Odds of Obtaining a Reservation

We've been purchasing the Timed Entry passes for three years now. And, we think we've developed a pretty good system for getting them. Our strategies and methods are included below.

First of all, if you haven't done so already, access the recreation.gov website, and sign up for an account. Don't wait. Do it now.

Visit https://recreation.gov
and create your account.

After setting up your account, perform a search on the site for **"Rocky Mountain National Park Timed Entry."**

When the RMNP Timed Entry page opens, look for the "**Favorite**" feature under the headline. Set this page as a favorite by selecting the heart icon. Then familiarize yourself with the rest of the website.

Now, here comes the "plan ahead" part.

Set reminders/alarms on your phone/tablet/computer (or all three) that will go off on the date(s) you need to buy your reservations. Set these alarms so they go off 10-15 minutes ahead of the start times for the types of ticket(s) you want to purchase.

As a reminder, next-day reservations go on sale at 7 pm MT on the previous day. Advanced purchase reservations go on sale at 8 am MT on the first day of the month preceding the month of the ticket.

We usually set two alarms for ticketing events – one an hour ahead of time and another 10 minutes ahead of time. This gives us time to ensure we're set up, connected, and ready to go.

While you're waiting for the start time, familiarize yourself with the decisions you'll need to make and how to make those decisions on the site itself.

• Which pass? (**Pack Access+** or **Park Access**)

• What date do you want to go?

• What time slot do you want?

Tickets go fast. Really fast. You'll need to be fast, too. Watch the minutes and the seconds count down.

Refresh Your Browser on the Hour!

When you see 6:59 pm MT change to 7:00 pm MT (for next-day reservations), or 7:59 am MT change to 8:00 am MT (for advanced purchase reservations) - refresh your browser immediately and keep doing it until the webpage updates.

Then start making your selection(s).

• First, choose the type of pass you want.

• Second, select the date you want.

• Third, select the time slot.

• Finally, select **Request Tickets** and hope for the best.

If you're lucky, you'll be taken to the Order Details page, where you can *Proceed to Cart* or *Continue Shopping*.

If you're not that lucky and receive the dreaded "The server is too busy, please try again." message, you'll need to start over by returning to the RMNP Timed Entry Reservation homepage and repeating the whole process. (This is when the aforementioned "Favorite" setting can help you a lot.)

We usually don't have too much trouble getting Advanced Purchase tickets using this method. However, getting the next-day tickets has been hit-and-miss for us. It's purely the luck of the draw based on the demand at that time.

By the way, you may have noticed that I said "we" and "us" above. When Emma and I want to obtain a Timed Entry Reservation, we are both accessing the site on our own devices simultaneously – thereby doubling our chances of success.

If we have friends or guests who also want to get in the park with us, we often share the same instructions with them to maximize our chances of getting in the park. However, keep in mind that the person named on the Timed Entry Reservation (the buyer of the ticket) must be with you to get into the park. Yes, the rangers will check your ID to ensure the rules are being followed.

Please Don't Blame the Rangers

In 2023, we were waiting in line at the Bear Lake Road entrance. It was a gorgeous morning! The line was 15-20 cars deep but was moving well ... until a vehicle two cars ahead of us reached the gate. Our windows were open, so we could hear a good portion of what the driver was saying to the ranger, and it wasn't nice at all.

Long story short, the driver didn't have the proper pass and was furious that he was being asked to turn around. When I say furious, I mean furious!

After a couple of minutes of his heated ranting at the ranger, he finally did the U-turn and left with his family in tow. When we pulled up to the gate, the emotional damage from that verbal assault was obvious, with tears welling up in the ranger's eyes.

We showed her our timed entry reservation and entry pass, and then paused briefly to offer some caring and supporting comments as well as two friendly smiles. Regardless, *her* gorgeous morning had been obliterated.

This was the worst behavior we've personally witnessed, but there have been numerous other times when the drivers thought it was important to share their "advice" with the rangers in a loud fashion.

We understand that certain individuals might be unhappy about the Timed Entry Reservation process. But, there's no call for being mean or rude to Rangers – or anyone for that matter. It's not the ranger's fault. They don't make the rules.

Chapter 6

Accessing RMNP Without a Timed Entry Reservation

There's always a workaround.

Even when you plan well and use our suggestions, there's a chance you might not be able to secure a Timed Entry Reservation. Don't give up! You still have a few available options to get you in the park without one.

Go Very Early in the Morning ... or Go Later.

RMNP is open 24 hours, seven days a week, 365 days a year. Gates are only closed for inclement weather, natural disasters, significant road repairs, or emergencies/rescues.

Entry passes are always required to enter and enjoy the park. However, you don't always need the elusive Timed Entry Reservation.

For example, you can enter the Bear Lake Road gate without the reservation before 5 am MT or after 6 pm MT. The rest of the park can be enjoyed without a Timed Entry Reservation as long as you enter before 9 am MT or after 2 pm MT.

RMNP's Hiker Shuttle Service

Hiker Shuttle

If you can get a seat on the Hiker Shuttle, you do not need a separate Timed Entry Reservation.

The Hiker Shuttle can be used to get from the Estes Park Visitor Center (just east of downtown) to the Park-and-Ride Transit Hub. That's right! Directly from the visitor center to the transit hub. Reservations are required for the Hiker Shuttle.

These reservations are only available on a next-day basis, starting at 5 pm MT. Like the Timed Entry Reservation, these tickets go fast!

Reservations can be obtained via
• Website: recreation.gov
• Recreation.gov mobile app
• Toll-free phone number: 877-444-6777
• Intl. Telephone: +1 606-515-6777
• TTD Telephone: 877-833-6777

For more info, please visit the Hiker Shuttle Reservation Website.

RMNP's In-Park Shuttle

Once you're in the park, you can hop a ride on RMNP's In-Park Shuttle.

There are two free in-park shuttle routes: One for Bear Lake Road and another for Moraine Park. These shuttles enable visitors to easily move between specific locations along the Bear Lake Road corridor and within Moraine Park.

Just make your way to the Park-and-Ride Transit Hub on Bear Lake Road and use that as your base. There's plenty of free parking and buses run regularly, so you'll be saving a good deal of time.

Reserve a Campsite Inside RMNP

Timed Entry Reservations are not required if you have reserved one of the campsites inside RMNP. You still need to pay the standard entry fee, but there's no reservation fee.

Most of these campsites can be reserved up to 6 months ahead of time. However, some are available on a short-term basis. And, if someone cancels, their campsite becomes immediately available.

Campground rentals start at $35 per night.

There are four campgrounds in RMNP: three on the east side and one on the west side. All of these campsites can be reserved via the following methods:
• Website: recreation.gov
• Recreation.gov mobile app
• Toll-free phone number: 877-444-6777
• Intl. Telephone: +1 606-515-6777
• TTD Telephone: 877-833-6777

Third-Party Guides and Vendors

There are quite a few local businesses and non-profits that provide guided tours and trips inside RMNP.

By being a customer of a permitted tour operator, you can have an enjoyable time inside RMNP without needing either the Entry Fee or the Timed Entry Reservation. Here are some to consider.

Rocky Mountain Conservancy (RMC)

The Rocky Mountain Conservancy (formerly known as the Rocky Mountain Nature Association) has been protecting RMNP for more than 90 years through trail maintenance, land protection, historic preservation, education, training, and stewardship. As part of their educational efforts, RMC offers a variety of guided tours led by naturalist guides ranging from 3-6 hours long.

♥ Highly Recommended

For more info, please refer to the Rocky Mountain Conservancy website.

Fishing Guides

If you book a guided fishing trip inside RMNP with an appropriately licensed vendor, you will not need a Timed Entry Reservation. You will, however, still need to get the general entry pass to enter RMNP.

In most cases, the guide will drive their own car/truck and you'll follow them in your vehicle. When the guide reaches the gate, they'll show their credentials/license to the ranger and then point out their client's vehicle (hopefully immediately behind them). And, that will get you through the gate and into the park.

We've typically fished in Moraine Park, which is inside the Bear Lake corridor. Once you're through the gate, you can stay in the Bear Lake Road portion of the park for the rest of the day as long as you don't leave the Bear Lake Road corridor. However, if you exit Bear Lake Road, you can still continue to enjoy the rest of the park with your general admission pass.

For our recommended fishing guides, please refer to the "Fishing" section of the chapter titled, "What Else Is There Do?."

Tour Companies

Using a tour company not only gets you into RMNP, but you also get to enjoy the ride and the scenery without needing to drive yourself!

We don't have any direct experience with the following vendors. However, we do see them in the park quite often.
• Green Jeep Tours
• Wildside 4x4 Tours
• Estes Park Guided Tours

Also, a special shout-out to KEP Expeditions and Full Potential Wilderness. These organizations offer specially designed tours that are inclusive and accessible for all guests.

For additional options, please refer to the Estes Park Visitor's Guide.

Chapter 7

Where are the Elk?

You never know where they'll show up next.

One of the most asked questions at the visitor center and through social media starts with, "Where can I see *<insert animal name here>*?"

We'll answer that question for you shortly, but let's cover some fun stuff first.

Fun Facts

We get a lot of "interesting" questions about local wildlife from our visitors, so let's first dispel a few of the more common misunderstandings.

These animals are not "allowed" or "encouraged" to exit the park or enter the town. They just go where they want when they want. They are wild animals.

We once heard a discussion between two visitors, where the following was uttered: "They only let the tame ones in town." To be totally clear, this is not accurate. These animals are not trained by park rangers, state wildlife officials, or town personnel.

The animals you see are not pets. The collars some of them wear are not shock collars. The collars are used by wildlife officials to track the animals so they can better monitor the herds.

Now that we've had a little laugh, let's talk safety.

Being Safe Around Wild Animals

Worth stating again. They are all wild animals. They may be somewhat accustomed to us humans, but they still need their space. That means you should carefully consider the distance between you and them at all times. If you have a dog with you, double or triple the amount of space.

These are all wild animals.
Powerful, strong, and dangerous.

Would it be cool to get a selfie with a massive bull elk? Sure!

But is that picture worth your life or that of a family member, or perhaps someone you don't even know? Is it worth the life of a majestic animal that may need to be put down as a result of attacking a human who ventured too close?

Simple answer: No, it is not.

No one likes to be told what to do. We get that. However, no human can outrun any of these animals, and you will not be able to protect yourself or your family members if they charge you. They are quick, powerful, strong, and dangerous.

Maintaining a long-distance relationship often works out quite well for everyone. Please give them a wide berth - for your safety and the safety of the animal.

Okay. Now that we're done with the nagging, let's get you pointed to the best places.

Note: The following recommendations are based on what we've personally seen and experienced over the last three decades. No promises or guarantees; just good places to start looking.

Elk

If Estes Park has an iconic animal, it is - without question - the elk. They can be seen/found almost anywhere in town. Downtown, by the lake, on the riverwalk, on either golf course, around the YMCA of the Rockies, along any road or highway, and at any elevation. Anywhere is open range for the elk. That said, here are some good places to start your search.

In the summer, many of the elk migrate to higher elevations where there is cooler weather and lots of food. This means there will be less of them in and around town. However, it is fairly common to see them in Moraine Park, Horseshoe Park, and anywhere along Fall River Road and Trail Ridge Road. It's also common to see them wading in Lake Estes, or in the pond next to Discovery Lodge.

In late summer or early fall, the elk rut begins. This is their mating season. Male elk (bulls) start gathering herds of females (cows) and moving them into the lower elevations. All mature bulls are feeling the same hormonal influences, so it's not unusual to see bulls sparring each other for the right to breed. (BTW, these hormonal changes can also make them more aggressive to humans.)

The bigger bulls amass the largest harems. But they're also constantly chasing off or battling other bulls, who are trying to gather their own harem.

Generally speaking, during the rut, the best place to see very large bulls (and their very large harems) is in Moraine Park inside RMNP. It's also fairly common to find one or more herds on Estes Park's nine-hole golf course (a short walk east of the Visitor Center), and on the 18-hole golf course east of Highway 7.

From the fall to the beginning of the next summer, these same animals can be found anywhere in the lower elevations. Below the Lake Estes dam, across Highway 36 from Lake Estes, YMCA of the Rockies, Fish Creek Road, Devils Gulch, anywhere along Highway 7, Mary's Lake Road, Beaver Meadows, Moraine Park … take your pick.

Moose

In the past, moose were more commonly seen on the west side of RMNP, just north of the Grand Lake entrance gate. That area remains a great place to see them. However, we've recently been seeing moose a lot more often on the Estes Park side of RMNP.

Moose love the water. And they're built for it. Their long legs allow them to wade through lakes, ponds, streams, or anything wet and filled with tasty water plants - their preferred food. So, focus your attention on the water corridors.

A great place to start a "moosin" adventure is Sheep Lakes. Sheep Lakes is named for the Rocky Mountain Big Horn Sheep that drop down from the upper elevations to drink water and lap the mud for its minerals. In 2020, many of us were seeing far more moose than sheep there, so we started (jokingly) referring to the lakes as Moose Lakes.

If they aren't at the lakes, you may want to follow the two primary water sources for Sheep Lakes. Try the open areas south of the Alluvial Fan Trail or go further west to the Endovalley Picnic Area. We've seen them lying in the shade between the picnic tables numerous times. Or, continue on Trail Ridge Road and then turn right at Deer Junction. Continue on Trail Ridge Road for about a mile and you'll see an open meadow on the south side of the road. Anywhere between that meadow and the Beaver Ponds is a great place to find moose.

Sprague Lake and Lilly Lake are also productive areas for seeing a moose or two, especially in the early mornings and around dusk. Though less common (so far), moose have also been seen along the streams in Moraine Park.

Moose have been seen in town (we even had one in our backyard), but they aren't nearly as common as elk.

Rocky Mountain Big Horn Sheep

We had been coming to RMNP for dozens of years before we actually saw any Big Horn Sheep. We waited for them at Sheep Lakes. We searched up and down the steeper cliffs to the north of Horseshoe Park, Alluvial Fan, and along Old Fall River Road. People talked about them often, but we were never in the right spot at the right time. Finally, on a trip here in April 2017, we found our groove.

The mating season for the Big Horn Sheep is in the late fall and early winter. Like the elk, the male sheep (rams) battle with other males to earn the right to mate with the females (ewes). Most of the time, they seem to be doing this on the cliffs at higher elevations, However, we came across a couple of these groupings along Fall River Road, just west of town.

We had seen lots of photos and videos of the Big Horn Rams, but nothing compares to seeing a big Ram in person. The first one we came across was incredible. Full spiral of the horns. Sizable, with a body made of lean, cut, body-builder muscle. He was magnificent (and frankly a little scary).

We're happy to report that we've been seeing more sheep more often since that trip. Probably just luck, but we aren't complaining.

For your best shot at seeing sheep on your visit, first try the aptly named Sheep Lakes, or anywhere along the steep hillside to the north of Sheep Lakes back to the Fall River Entrance gate. They're also fairly common on the steep cliffs along Highway 34, east of

Drake and west of Loveland. By the way, even if you don't see any sheep, the canyon itself is incredibly scenic.

Other Notable Critters

Elk, moose, and big horns are the top three, but here are some others to watch for.

Mule Deer

Mule deer are a common sight in and around Estes Park and RMNP. Second to elk in number, mule deer frequently occupy the same feeding grounds. However, they rarely mingle outside of their own herds.

They're frequent visitors to our neighborhood and many others in town. But they're also commonly seen on Trail Ridge Road just east of the aptly named Deer Junction, or anywhere along the Bear Lake Corridor

Bears

Yes, we have bears, Black Bears to be specific. They may not always be black in color, but they're all Black Bears. No grizzlies (so far). They're pretty reclusive, but they are out there. They love to eat our garbage, which is why many of us have bear-resistant garbage containers.

There really isn't one place where we see them consistently or predictably. However, you try to catch a glimpse of them west of Sheep Lakes, in Moraine Park, or (again) in any backyard.

In 2014, one of our local bears walked through Lonigan's Saloon, Nightclub & Grill, located in the heart of downtown Estes Park. The bear simply entered the back door, sauntered through the dining area, and then walked out the front door. Following this, Lonigan's declared itself the "Best Bear Bar". Don't believe us? Check out the video on YouTube.

Mountain Lions

They've probably always lived in and around Estes Park due to the ample supply of food (aka deer, elk, etc.) However, the proliferation of video doorbells has certainly corroborated their existence in modern days.

They're seldom seen in daylight, but rest assured, these animals are like ninjas. The homes on Prospect Mountain (the big hill just south of downtown) seem to record quite a few visits from these big cats. But these animals could be anywhere at any time.

Coyotes

These crafty canines can be found anywhere in Estes Park or RMNP. More often than not, you'll hear them howling in the early morning when the pack gets back together after a night of hunting. Not a big threat to humans, but keep your pets on a leash when you're walking outside.

Wolves

We've heard of several wolf sightings recently, especially in the northern part of RMNP. Many say these eyewitnesses are wrong –

that they saw coyotes – not wolves. We haven't seen any wolves ourselves, but that doesn't mean they aren't out there.

The official reintroduction of wolves to Colorado started in December 2023, so it's only a matter of time for them to show up.

Bobcats

Again, another elusive feline predator in the Rocky Mountains. The first one we saw was crossing the road just north of Lyons on Highway 34. The most recent sighting for us was just outside our front door a few weeks ago. They're about twice the size of a common house cat, but meeting one face-to-face remains a little intimidating.

Marmots (Yellow-bellied Marmots)

Technically, they're the largest members of the squirrel family. However, they look more like large gophers, woodchucks, or beavers (without the tail). They love to live and burrow among our many rock piles, so Estes Park and RMNP are ideal locations for them.

The Estes Park Waste Transfer Station is home to a few, and you may find others throughout town. However, you'll find a lot more in the higher elevations on trails or along Old Fall River Road.

There's also a large colony on the cliff immediately east of the gift shop at the Alpine Visitor Center. (You'll probably need to be in the store to see them up close as the cliff edge is quite steep.)

Pikas

Pikas (pronounced pie•kas) are small rodents about the size of a very small rabbit, but with shorter ears that are more round. Like the marmots, they like to live and forage among the many rock piles at higher elevations.

If you come upon some, you may be alerted to their presence by their high-pitched alarm call (kind of like a chirp), which they use to warn each other about possible predators. We haven't seen any in town, but we've seen numerous colonies at Trail Ridge Road, especially at Forest Canyon Overlook and Rockcut.

Birds

Everything and every size - from Bald Eagles, hawks, turkeys, owls, woodpeckers, perchers, and a wide range of songbirds ... all the way down to four different species of hummingbirds, they're all here at some point in the year. We even had a flock of pelicans on Lake Estes in 2023.

Snakes

In our 30 years here, we've never seen a snake in Estes Park or RMNP. As we understand things, the elevation is too high for rattlesnakes and the only other likely candidate is the common garter snake – a very small and harmless fellow (unless you get a heart attack when you see any snake.) So, rest easy.

Everything Else

For the most in-depth guide to all of the mammals, birds, amphibians, reptiles, and insects in RMNP, please visit the National Park's very own "critter catalog" at https://irma.nps.gov/NPSpecies/Search/SpeciesList/ROMO.

Bigfoot

We've never seen a bigfoot in the area. So, we can't point you to a likely place to see one. However, there is an active Bigfoot contingent in the Estes Park area. We even have an annual Big Foot Days event in April. See the chapter titled, "Estes Park Events."

Chapter 8

Eating in Estes Park

We only mention the places we like.

Everybody needs to eat, and the first questions we usually hear are "Where's a good place to eat?" or "Where can I get a good <insert favorite food here.>" Don't worry, we've got you covered.

By the way, you don't always need to dine out. We have quite a few alternative suggestions for you in the chapter titled, "Insider Tips for Saving Money (and Time)".

Our Criteria

This chapter contains the names of places where *we* like to eat in Estes Park – places that we frequent and recommend to our friends and families. We understand this may be fairly subjective, so here's how we decide which ones to include.

We're very picky.

In addition to our many years of food consumption, we also have more than a decade of hands-on experience working in the restaurant industry – cooking, serving, tending bar, and management. We understand the business. And that's why we're very picky in choosing where we go and what we eat or drink while there.

Here's what we look for.

First and foremost, cleanliness.
Don't seat us at a dirty (or wet) table. Don't hand us a sticky menu. I don't want to see my server's thumb sticking in my mashed potatoes when they place my plate on the table. And I really don't want to see black spots (mold) in my ice cubes, nor lipstick on my wine glass.

Quality
The food tastes great. The food is still warm when it gets to the table (salads not included). The burger (or steak) is cooked correctly. The order is complete. You don't feel sick two hours after eating it.

Service
You know great service when you get it. You're greeted with a smile when you sit down. You get what you ordered. The server returns to your table to see how things are going after service. Your tab is presented promptly. Maybe they even remember your name on your third or fourth visit.

Value
How do you feel when you leave? Was it worth going? Did you get your money's worth? Are you glad you went? Would you tell your friends about it?

Consistency
We understand how hard it is to find and keep good employees

in Estes Park. With that in mind, we're willing to overlook certain things from time to time. However, this factor trips up a lot of dining experiences for us. We're paying our hard-earned dollars for this meal and we want a great experience EVERY time we go. If it's hit-and-miss, we're less likely to recommend it.

The restaurants we present in the following pages have lived up to those criteria during our visits.

If you don't see a restaurant listed here, it doesn't mean it's bad. It only means that it didn't make the list ... this time. Many of the dining options in Estes Park are truly right on the cusp of doing everything right (see comment above about "consistency).

We've tried a lot of the dining opportunities in Estes Park, but we have not tried them all. So, there may be some restaurants that didn't make the list simply because we haven't been there yet. There are no restaurants that we refuse to visit or revisit. In fact, we revisit restaurants with the hopes that they've improved. Regardless, we won't say anything bad about the places that we would not recommend.

> "If you can't say anything nice,
> don't say anything at all."
> -- Mom --

One last point. We pay full price when we dine. We are not compensated in any way, shape, or form to recommend certain dining options in our reviews. These are our personal, unbiased and honest reviews based on our own experiences.

Let's get started. Here are the places we really like, sorted by their respective category.

Breakfast / Brunch

We love going out for brunch! If you can judge a place by how many people are waiting in line, then these places deserve your attention.

Notchtop Bakery and Café

Notchtop offers breakfast and lunch, but not dinner. Their menu is rich with options, but don't expect just the standard fares. They have five different Eggs Benedict varieties, four unique French toast plates, five hashes, and even more omelets. Dine inside, on their small patio, or grab it to go.

Our favorite items: Sundance Mountain Benedict, Country Benedict, Mexican Omelet, Chicken Fried Steak and Eggs. Did we mention their Mimosas, Bloody Marys, and the Micheladas?

♥ Highly Recommended

Mountain Home Café

Located in the same parking lot as Notchtop and usually with an equally long waiting line, Mountain Home Café is a worthy competitor. They offer a slightly smaller menu but everything we've eaten has been delicious. Dine inside, on their small patio, or grab it to go.

Our favorite items: Arizona Hashbrowns, Mexican Benedict, and the Swirled Cinnamon French Toast.

♥ Highly Recommended

Egg of Estes

Their tagline is "Home cooking away from home." That's a really good way to describe it. Even though our moms never made a lot of their offerings, you can taste the passion they put into their food (and their service). Quick, clean, and delicious. Dine in or order it to go.

Our favorite items: Classic B&G with Eggs, Avocado Smash Egg Sandwich, and the Huevo Rancheros.

♥ Highly Recommended

Cinnamon's Bakery

Since it opened in 2016, Cinnamon's Bakery has been our de facto standard for the best cinnamon roll in town. Selection is limited to only a few different varieties, but all are delicious.

We have a friend that calls them, "Sold Out Cinnamon Rolls" ... if that's any indication of how good they are. So, to claim your share, get there early. Or call ahead and they'll box some up for you before they all disappear. There is some seating inside, but most people just get them to go.

♥ Highly Recommended

Here are a couple more breakfast faves to consider ...

Big Horn Restaurant

If you want big and good pancakes, this is the place! Lots of other great food, too. When we first started coming here more than 20 years ago, we always asked for our favorite server. She owns the place today!

Fresh Burger Stop

You'll see Fresh Burger Stop at the top of our list of best burgers (see below). Yes, their burgers are great, but their breakfast burritos are really good, too.

Burgers

Since the pandemic, it seems like $20 (or more) burgers are trending everywhere. That's a little pricey for most of us. So, here are three outstanding options, and a couple more – all with reasonable prices and great tasting burgers.

Fresh Burger Stop

Located inside the Sinclair Gas Station on Highway 36 (just before the Beaver Meadows entrance to RMNP), this is **one of the two go-to burger shacks for locals**.

Great quality. Reasonable prices. Quick turnaround. Everything is served to go. Drive-thru and walk up.

♥ Highly Recommended

Boss Burgers & Gyros

Located across the street from Fresh Burger, Boss Burgers & Gyros are neck-and-neck in price, quality and taste. Again, locals love it for many of the same reasons.

Great quality. Lots of options. Reasonable prices. Quick turnaround. Limited seating. Drive-thru, to-go, and walk up.

♥ Highly Recommended

Penelope's Old Time Burgers

If you're downtown and need a burger, this is a really good place to go.

Great quality. Lots of options. Quick turnaround. To-go or dine-in.

♥ Highly Recommended

The Wapiti Colorado Pub (also listed in "Full-Service Dining")

Great food (especially the burgers). Lots of options, including many unique fares. Meticulously clean. Great bartenders, servers, cooks, and management. Excellent food. Consistently great. Reasonable prices.

♥ Highly Recommended

Grubsteak

We're pretty sure this downtown restaurant was there on one of our first trips to Estes Park, but we didn't start going there until recently. Silly us.

Ask for the Yak burger! You won't be disappointed.

Lonigan's

Remodeled in 2022/2023, this downtown Irish-themed establishment does a great job with its burgers. Lots of other options, too. Great service. Reasonable prices.

Pizza

One truly outstanding option and a couple more

Antonio's Real NY Pizza

Located on Highway 34 east of downtown, Antonio's has been serving the Estes Park region since 2014. The owner (Antonio) is a "real" New Yorker and a member of the World Pizza Champions! It shows in his work, too.

Great quality. Worth the slightly higher price. Call ahead for takeout or dine-in. Beer and wine are available. You may even get served by their robot!

♥ Highly Recommended

During the pandemic, many locals were out of work or, at best, struggling to keep their families fed. Antonio went above and beyond in providing milk, eggs, homemade bread, and more to many locals who desperately needed them. We're proud to recommend this community-minded restaurant.

Sweet Basilco

Check out the "Italian" category below for more info on Sweet Basilico. Like all of their other dishes, they do great pizzas, too!

Poppy's Pizza and Grill

Poppy's menu extends beyond its core of Italian-inspired fares, but the pizza is legit.

Deli/Sandwiches

Country Market

Inside The Country Market is a fantastic deli with a wide variety of meats, cheeses, soups, salads, and, of course, sandwiches.

Chester's Philly

We love, love, love a good cheesesteak, and Chester's fits the bill. Soft roll, tasty meat, just the right amount of cheese. Everything is cooked to order. They've got other stuff, too, but we only focus on the cheesesteaks.

Dine in or takeout.

General/American

The Wapiti Colorado Pub

One of our favorite full-service restaurants in Estes Park.

In 2023, Wapiti moved from downtown to Nikki's Resort on Fall River Road. At first, we were worried that things might change, but they have continued to amaze us on every visit.

Great food (especially the burgers). Lots of options, including many unique fares. Meticulously clean. Great bartenders, servers, cooks, and management. Reasonable prices.

Our favorite items: Anything with "Slow Beef" in its name, Gyro Tacos, Fish Tacos, Rueben, Sloppy Joe, and many more. Their prime rib is to die for, too.

♥ Highly recommended

The Rock Inn

It took us a few years to "discover" The Rock Inn, but we're huge fans now. Very nice food selection. Great quality. Really attentive and skilled servers and bartenders. Live music, too!

Our favorite items: The Devils on Horseback appetizer (order two if there are more than two people at your table), Bison Meatballs, Stroganoff, and Mediterranean Pasta. The Bread Pudding is awesome, too.

♥ Highly recommended

Bird & Jim

Every meal we've had here has been delicious. The chefs (and the servers and bartenders) know what they're doing. Great Happy Hour, too. If it weren't for the limited parking and line at the door, we'd go to Bird & Jim a lot more often.

Our favorite items: The Mountain Jim Burger, Cast-iron Roasted Half Chicken, and their Happy Hour.

Asian

China Garden

Quite simply, the best Chinese (and some Thai) in town. Everything served to go. No delivery.

Estes Thai

Just what you'd expect at your favorite Thai place in your hometown ... traditional Thai dishes with varying levels of spice to meet everyone's needs. Dine-in, takeout, and delivery.

Nepal's Café

We weren't familiar with Nepalese food until our daughter insisted on dining there. Very glad we went. Lots of curries and momos, and several naan options, too. Dine-in or takeout. No delivery.

Italian

Sweet Basilico

The first time we went to Sweet Basilco, it was really busy. The hostess told us we could wait or she could seat us at the bar. We generally like sitting at the bar, so we took her up on that option. Turns out this wasn't the bar where they make drinks. This was a pair of seats right in front of the kitchen where you could watch the chefs do their magic. It was the Chef's Bar!

As a former short-order cook in college, I loved every minute of it. Emma probably would have preferred a more romantic table, but she came around when the chefs started randomly sliding tasting plates in front of us – some items right off the menu as well as other custom creations we think they made just for us. This is one of the most fun dining experiences in my life.

We'd describe their cuisine as high-quality, old-school Italian. Traditional and excellent. Reservations are a must during the busy season.

BTW, they have 3 Tesla destination chargers on-premise, so you can satisfy your hunger and recharge your EV at the same time.

Our favorite items: Fried Raviolis, Spaghetti Carbonara, Veal Marsala, and any pizza!

♥ Highly Recommended

Mexican

Ed's Cantina & Grill

Ed's was a favorite of ours since one of first trips to Estes Park. Fantastic burgers, giant burritos, and more. The building, décor, and menu (and owners) have all changed a lot since then, but we still love everything about Ed's. Tasty food. Great selection. Have you ever had an avocado margarita? Try one for a very tasty surprise.

Reasonable prices. Skilled, friendly bartenders. They also cater! Parking can be tough, but if you parked at the Visitor Center, it's a short walk.

Our favorite items: Any of their tacos, Bison Enchiladas, Queso/chips, Avocado Margaritas (not a typo – there's actually avocado in the margarita).

Fine Dining

Sometimes you just want to splurge on a really good meal. Here you go ...

Twin Owls Steakhouse

Escape from the downtown hustle and bustle, and treat yourself to what we consider the best fine-dining restaurant in Estes Park.

Located in the Tahara Lodge complex off Highway 7, Twin Owls offers a wide variety of exactly what you'd expect at a world-class steakhouse. Burrata Caprese and Bacon-Wrapped Scallops headline the appetizer list for us while the chefs are preparing the beef, elk, bison, pork, and salmon entrees on the grill. Need a lobster tail with that? No problem.

Full bar and loaded wine list. Superb service. Great views! Call ahead for reservations.

Our favorite items: Braised Short Ribs, Prime Rib, and any beef entrée served "Twin Sister Style" (with Béarnaise sauce, blue cheese, pistachios, and green onions).

♥ Highly Recommended

Hunter's Chophouse

Everything about Hunter's Chophouse screams fine dining. From the dry-aged Black Angus Rib Eye, Roasted Bone Marrow, and Bison Oscar Sirloin to the Duck Ragu and Kobe Beef burgers, you will not be disappointed.

In addition to being recognized by Wine Spectator with their Award of Excellence, they also host wine-pairing dinners from time to time.

Skilled chefs and servers. Always a line, so call ahead for reservations.

Our favorite items: Rib Eye, Filet Mignon, basically anything that's medium rare.

In Their Own Category

We're not sure how to categorize these, but we do enjoy them often.

You Need Pie

They may have started as a pie shop, but they're much more now. This self-proclaimed "diner" not only offers obligatory (and delicious) pies and baked goods, but they've also expanded their menu to include a wide variety of options for breakfast, lunch, and dinner. They also cater!

Our favorite items: Oinker Biscuit (breakfast), Val's meatloaf, and way too many great desserts to name.

Even though she competes with all of them, the owner of You Need Pie is a wonderful leader among Estes Park's eateries. Val demonstrates this every year by organizing "Estes Park Dine Around", a month-long event in April where local restaurants offer "small plates" and beverages at reduced rates so locals (and visitors) can sample their menu and sing their praises.

♥ Highly Recommended

The Donut Haus

When we first started coming to Estes Park, we were told about the great donuts and donut holes being sold out of a tiny shack at the corner of Moraine Avenue and Crags Drive. The "building" was indeed incredibly small and had only a few parking spaces, but they cranked out some fantastic donuts!

The original building was recently demolished to enable "The Loop" bypass project, but the donuts live on at the new Donut Haus inside the Sinclair Gas Station, a little farther west of its original spot. BTW, this is the same gas station with one of the best burgers in town – Fresh Burgers.

♥ Highly Recommended

The Taffy Shop®

Okay. Maybe this isn't "dining", but you still need to give The Taffy Shop a try.

There are several places to buy saltwater taffy in Estes Park, but this one is the original and the best. Established in 1935 at the same location they're in today, using the same recipes and some of the same machinery. If it ain't broke, don't fix it. (Our words, not theirs.)

Breweries (Beer)

Lots of places sell beer. We have three favorites that actually make their own.

Rock Cut Brewing Company

Our favorite. Very much a local's place, but plenty of smart visitors make their way here, too. They serve an excellent and wide-ranging variety of brews. Served cold by friendly and knowledgeable beer tenders. Creative swag. Small patio outside.

♥ Highly Recommended

Avant Garde

Generally speaking, they have a slightly smaller selection than Rock Cut, but are equally good at their craft. Mostly outside seating, but they do have a few tables inside. Perfect place to relax after a long hike in RMNP!

Lumpy Ridge

No table service, no frills, but great beer. That's all we need.

BTW, if you see the **On The Hook** food truck here, you'd be really smart to try their awesome fish and chips along with a Lumpy Ridge brew.

Lumpy Ridge opened a second location – a "tasting room" – downtown at the end of 2023.

The Barrel

To be clear, The Barrel is not a brewery. But it still deserves recognition for its large selection of beer. At last count, they were serving more than 50 beers, ales, pilsners, porters, and IPAs, and more, plus gluten-free and non-alcoholic. There's something here that will surely please everyone in your group.

Coffee

If you don't include the "Green Mermaid" chain, Estes Park has more than a dozen coffee shops. We've only been to a few, and these are the two we like the most.

Coffee on the Rocks

Like all of our faves, the coffee and the service are really good here (the limited food items, too). However, the ambiance of being right next to the river is what keeps us coming back.

It's super chill and so relaxing. Feed the ducks and geese that gather around the pond. Or sit in an Adirondack chair and read a book. Bask in the sun. Meditate to the sounds of the river. It's just a great start or finish to any day.

♥ Highly Recommended

Inkwell and Brew

Downstairs is a retail shop with lots of thoughtful and artful items for writing and displaying. However, upstairs is where you go for beverages, games, and camaraderie. Our daughter and three close friends spent hours together here throughout their last week-long visit.

Whiskey Bars

Wapiti Colorado Pub

We've already mentioned the Wapiti Pub for its great burgers and its full-service dining. Well, they also have an excellent selection of whiskeys ... *and* bartenders who are happy to describe any of them for you.

♥ Highly Recommended

The Whiskey Bar and Cascades Restaurant (Inside the Stanley Hotel)

If you're looking for the widest selection, this is the place to go. Bartender knowledge may be a little hit-and-miss, but if you know what you want, that doesn't really matter now does it?

Lonigan's Irish Pub

As an Irish-themed bar, you'd expect a variety of Irish whiskey at Lonigan's. Well, you'd be right! However, they also have a couple dozen other whiskeys to tempt your palette.

The Whiskey Warmup

Okay, this isn't a bar or restaurant. It's an event. But it definitely deserves a mention on this list.

Every March, whiskey distillers from all around come to downtown Estes Park to show off their wares. We haven't missed one of these events since they started.

Designated drivers are suggested. Tickets are limited. (See the chapter titled, " Estes Park Events.")

♥ Highly Recommended

Chapter 9

Must-See Destinations

There's a lot of 'em!

So many to choose from. Here are our faves, grouped into various regions. By the way, everything in this chapter is ♥ Highly Recommended

In RMNP

We think everything in RMNP is a must-see. Every time we go there, our awe of the beauty never changes. That said, here are some of our favorite spots.

Bear Lake Road Corridor

As mentioned earlier, this is a very desirable part of RMNP. It's an easy drive full of scenic views, and you'll have access to lots of lakes and trailheads.

Sprague Lake

Easy half-mile hike around the lake. Good spot to look for moose or fly fish for trout. Not uncommon to see weddings happening on the north side of the lake during summer and fall. When you're on the backside of the lake, you'll enjoy a particularly gorgeous panorama of Hallett Peak and the Tyndale Glacier. Fairly generous parking area with bathrooms and picnic tables.

Bear Lake

Located at the end of the road, Bear Lake has a fairly large parking lot that is almost always full. That's because (a) the trail around Bear Lake is fairly easy and (b) there are so many other trailheads here.

The Dream Lake Trail is a great starter where you'll pass Nymph Lake, Dream Lake, and (if you have the stamina) Emerald Lake. Or take the Lake Haiyaha Trail, or head to Mills Lake or Alberta Falls. You get the point. Lots of options. Refer to your trail maps for more.

Trail Ridge Road

Trail Ridge Road starts in Horseshoe Park just west of Sheep Lakes. It then climbs to the Alpine Visitor Center, and eventually descends into Grand Lake on the west side. So much to see.

Trail Ridge Road closes during the winter due to the deep snow. However, it usually remains open and accessible on the east side up to Many Parks Curve or Rainbow Curve.

Sheep Lakes

These are two small lakes (most of you might call them ponds) a short drive after you enter the park at the Fall River Entrance.

They offer a nice foreground to the mountains that rise beyond. However, more importantly, it's the wildlife these lakes attract that make this worth a stop. We regularly see elk, moose, sheep, turkeys, coyotes, bears, and more.

As you continue uphill, Beaver Ponds is a nice stop. It's a good spot to see moose, too. In the winter, Hidden Valley has a great sledding hill.

Many Parks Curve and Rainbow Curve

These two switchbacks have limited parking, but provide outstanding overlooks to Beaver Meadows, Moraine Park, and the Estes Valley (Many Parks Curve), or the Fall River Valley (Rainbow Curve).

Above Tree Line

Heading uphill, you'll soon reach the tree line, where nothing but AMAZING panoramas are sure to astound. Forest Canyon Overlook, Rock Cut, Gore Range Overlook, and, ultimately, the Alpine Visitor Center. Stopping at any of these overlooks defines "Must-See" and is certainly worth your time.

Rock Cut has a great trail into the alpine tundra with some mushroom-shaped rock formations at the end. It's a little steep at first, but then it levels off. Also, there's an active Pika community just north of the parking area.

In addition to the NPS interpretive center, the **Alpine Visitor Center** has a large parking area, a gift shop with limited dining options, and a separate outbuilding for bathrooms.

There's also the Alpine Ridge Trail, a steep, .6-mile which takes hikers to the pinnacle of the mountain. Remember, the elevation here is 11,750 feet above sea level. Breathing can be a challenge if you're out of shape or unaccustomed to the altitude.

Medicine Bow Curve

Sure, you just parked at the Alpine Visitor Center and saw some great views. However, this is worth the stop as the last "big view" from altitude on the way to Grand Lake.

Poudre Lake/Continental Divide

Poudre is a beautiful mountain lake. Take a short stroll while you're there to straddle the continental divide – where all water to the east drains into the Atlantic Ocean (or the Gulf of Mexico) and all water to the west drains to the Pacific Ocean. Good spot to hop on the Ute Pass or Milner Pass trails.

Fairview Curve

The pullout at Fairview Curve provides a great panoramic view of the Kawuneeche Valley and the Never Summit Range beyond. A series of switchbacks on the downhill side brings you to lower elevations rather quickly.

The valley's landscape remains beautiful from here to Grand Lake, but nothing quite as spectacular as the views at the top. That said, your chances of seeing moose anywhere in the valley are excellent!

Old Fall River Road (open only during summer months)

Old Fall River Road is the original road between Estes Park to the Alpine Visitor Center.

This gravel and dirt road is about 11 miles long and travel is one-way only (uphill). Once you start up the road, there's no turning back. Switchbacks abound. (Leave the big rigs and trailers at home.) Also, some great views! We love driving up Old Fall River Road!

Chasm Falls

Watch for the sign and parking area a mile or so after you pass the Endovalley Picnic Area. Then, park the car and take the short (and somewhat steep) trail to the bottom of the falls. Great spot for a family photo with the waterfalls as a backdrop.

Picnic Stops

The speed limit is only 15 mph on Old Fall River Road, so we're very casual when motoring up to the top. As such, it's fairly common for us the bring the proverbial picnic basket and then park the car at one of the many pullouts. There's one spot right above the switchbacks that we love. No picnic tables, no trash cans, no bathrooms. Just us and nature. A couple of folding chairs help, too.

Above Tree Line

As you get closer to the top, the trees fade away and the incredible panoramas abound. Lots of things to love up here! Many great spots to take a family portrait or lay out a picnic blanket. Just make sure the marmots don't steal your food!

In Town

The Stanley Hotel

There are two fairly iconic views most people associate with Estes Park. The first is the view of downtown with the mountains behind it. The second is just about any view of the white hotel with a red roof on the hill - The Stanley Hotel.

The hotel offers a stunning view from just about anywhere south and east of the city. Close up, far away, it doesn't really matter. The views inside are pretty amazing as well.

BTW, don't miss the rock formations just north of the Stanley. Those are Twin Owls.

The River Walk

The City of Estes Park is formed at the confluence of two rivers: Fall River and the Big Thompson River. Ultimately, the water feeds into Lake Estes, but only after passing through downtown. In the past few years, the Town and business owners decided to embrace this beautiful water feature and started adding paved walkways, outdoor seating, and rear entries for the many shops.

As outstanding as the River Walk is in the spring, summer, and fall, it is a beautiful wonderland in the winter. The Town does a stellar job of hanging LED lights – not too many, not too few. If you're here in November, December, or January, do yourself a favor and take your family portrait here.

The Knoll-Willows Open Space

Immediately across Highway 34 from the Stanley Hotel is the Knoll-Willows Open Space. Take a short and gentle hike to the south from this point and you'll eventually come to the edge of the hill, which lies right above the library and city hall. From there, you'll see a fantastic view of downtown as well as a panorama of the mountains beyond.

BTW, at one point in time, this open space was almost an outlet mall. Thanks to the actions taken by our former citizens, this land is now public space owned and managed by the Town of Estes Park.

The Estes Park Tram (New Owner!)

This gondola just south and west of downtown provides an awesome view from the top. Even though the Estes Park Tram was closed in 2023, we understand a new owner has taken over the business and plans to reopen in 2024. As of the publishing date, it remains closed. But we'll update this book as soon as we learn when/if it's running again. Fingers crossed.

Nearby

The Chapel on the Rock

As you're driving towards Estes Park on Hwy. 7, keep both hands on the wheel as you get closer to Longs Peak. You're about to be astonished by a small church on the west side of the road that looks like it was built right on top of a giant rock formation. Guess what? It was.

Its official name is **St. Catherine of Siena Chapel**. However, you may also hear it called Saint Catherine's Chapel on Rock, Chapel on the Rock at Camp St. Malo, or simply the Chapel on the Rock.

This is a functioning Catholic church that is operated and maintained by the Catholic Archdiocese of Denver. Blessed by Pope John Paul II during a visit in 1993, this church is open to the public for praying or just admiration. Parking is limited, but it's worth the trip inside.

Estes Park Welcome Sign

When you top the last hill coming into town from Lyons on Highway 36, you'll be greeted with a wonderful view of the Estes Valley and the **Welcome to Estes Park** sign.

For you selfie artists, this is the first of many opportunities you'll have to do selfie pics. Spoiler alert: The entrance gates to RMNP are also used a lot for this same purpose.

The Elk Rut

This isn't really a place or destination. However, it is a must-see event. Massive bull elk do battle with other bull elk so they can have mating rights for the next generation. It's one thing to see these guys on YouTube. It's a completely different thing to see it in person.

For more info, please refer to the chapter titled, "Where are the Elk?"

Chapter 10

Insider Tips for Saving Money (and Time)

Keep more of the green in your pocket.

Vacations in Estes Park can be expensive, but there are several ways to keep more of that green stuff in your own pockets.

Alternatives to Dining Out

As we all know, eating out is expensive, especially for families. Consider the following options to save some of your hard-earned cash.

Cook It Yourself

Next time you're looking for a place to stay, consider asking the following questions to help defray some of your food expenses:

- Is there a refrigerator?

- Is there a microwave?

- What about a full kitchen or kitchenette?

- Is there an outdoor grill you can use?

We really like to cook. So, it was not uncommon for us (as visitors) to book a place that had some form of a kitchen. Most were pretty small and had limited cookware, but they usually had enough to make easy meals like spaghetti, meatloaf, or a basic casserole. If they had an outdoor grill, hamburgers or steaks were usually on the menu. And, having a full-size refrigerator in the room made it easy to stock up on drinks, snacks, fruit, and sandwich meats we could pack up for hiking trips or picnics in RMNP.

Buy (or bring your own) plastic wrap, foil, paper plates, etc. to save even more on costs as well as clean-up time.

Foods To Go

If you don't feel like cooking, place a to-go order at your favorite restaurant. You'll save a ton of time by not waiting in line, as well as not waiting for service once you are seated! You'll also save money by not buying as much impulse food, such as appetizers or desserts, or cocktails/wine/beer.

When it's time to pick up your to-go order, consider having one person take the role as the designated driver while another goes into the restaurant to pay and carry out the package. That way, the driver can circle the block instead of trying (endlessly) to find a parking place.

Or, if you're already downtown but ready to head back to the hotel, consider picking up a to-go order from your favorite restaurant before returning to your parked car.

Grocery Stores

Grocery stores offer many options for food on the go. Ready-made sandwiches, pot pies, fried chicken, salads, fruit bowls, sushi, and more. If that's not enough, the freezer section is always filled with microwavable options.

Don't forget the drinks, too. Especially the adult beverages. You'll pay around $12 for a decent six-pack of beer in the grocery stores as compared to $8-15 per bottle/can at a restaurant (plus tip).

Delivery

As far as we can tell, Domino's Pizza and Jimmy Johns are the only places in town with dedicated delivery. However, many restaurants use third-party services to handle their deliveries, including Door Dash, Uber Eats, and Warrior Express. Check the restaurant's website to see which works best for you.

Groceries

Go to the grocery store on the way here.

Estes Park has two primary grocery stores: Safeway and The Country Market. (See the chapter titled, "Estes Park Essentials: Groceries" for additional options.)

They're both great stores, but the products they stock are often more expensive than your local home stores. And, they're always very busy during the peak season.

Very, very busy.

You'll likely end up going to one or both of these stores if you're here for more than a few days, but you can save yourself a lot of money (and time) by doing at least some of your grocery shopping *before* you get to Estes Park.

Longmont and Loveland are the closest cities with larger grocery stores. You probably drove through one of these cities on your way here.

BTW, if you do need to pick up some groceries while you're here, don't wait until the last minute. In fact, try to avoid the grocery stores (and their parking lots), between 9 am and 8 pm. It's not uncommon for the self-check line at Safeway to reach all of the way to the back of the store during peak visitation season.

Safeway opens at 6 am. Country Market at 7 am. Just sayin' ...

Bonus Savings Tip for Safeway Shoppers ... check the back of your receipt for coupons. On our last trip there (this morning), the coupons included discounts for Fresh Burger (the best burgers in town), Dominos, Jimmy John's, and Longhorn Liquor. (BTW, if your receipt tape is too short to show all of the coupons, press the button on the printer to run out more receipt tape so you can see all of the coupons.)

Gas/Fuel for Your Vehicle

Gas prices are far more expensive in Estes Park ... often $0.50 to $1.00 more per gallon. If you plan on spending any time driving in RMNP (doesn't everyone?), do yourself a favor and top off your tank in Longmont, Lyons, or Loveland (or Granby if you're on the west side).

Chapter 11

Estes Park Events

There's always something going on.

There's always something going on in Estes Park. Music, art shows, crafts, RMNP events, classes, and more. It would be impractical to try to include everything in this book, but here's a short list of some of the major events every year.

For more details and even more events, please refer to the Estes Park Online Visitors Guide or the Estes Park Events Complex. Our newspapers (the *Estes Park News* and the *Estes Park Trail-Gazette*) can help you plan as well.

Estes Park Wine and Chocolate Festival (February)

Roughly timed to coincide with Valentine's Day, this decadent festival is sure to delight. Hosted at the Estes Park Convention Center, this event sells out fast. (This is the first of three wine-related events in Estes Park each year.)

Whiskey Warmup (March)

Yeah, it's March. It's still cold and likely snowing. And this event is held outdoors. Don't worry, you'll warm up fast after tasting whiskies from a wide variety of distillers. Live music, too. This is a don't-miss event for us.

Heads Up: This event is usually held along the Riverwalk. However, for 2024, it's been moved to Bond Park due to complications with the ongoing construction of The Loop.

♥ Highly Recommended

Frozen Dead Guy Days (March)

Originally held in Nederland, CO, the Frozen Dead Guy Days festival "loosely" celebrates the life, er, death and cryopreservation of Bredo Morstoe. Bizarre, right? See Wikipedia for more info.

This fan-favored festival moved to Estes Park in 2023, and now includes Coffin Races, a Polar Plunge, three stages of music, and much, much more.

♥ Highly Recommended

Bigfoot Days (April)

Resident characters and appearances from guest experts bring Bigfoot to life for believers and non-believers alike in Bond Park. You can enjoy axe throwing, a climbing wall, food trucks, beers, and ... if you're lucky ... maybe a rare glimpse of the beast himself!

Estes Park Duck Race Festival (Early May)

It may sound a little silly to launch thousands of small rubber duckies into the river and see which one gets downtown first. But, it's actually a lot of fun!

Live music. Awesome prizes. And all proceeds go to local charities. (Note: Every single rubber duck is accounted for when the race is over.)

♥ Highly Recommended

Estes Park Wool Market (early June)

If you're interested in wool and other animal fibers, this event covers everything from Alpacas to the petting Zoo.

Watch and learn through workshops and demonstrations covering shearing, carding, felting, weaving, and making yarn from angora rabbits, cashmere goats, llamas, sheep, and more. Be sure to save time for the sheep-dog presentations.

Scandinavian Midsummer Festival (Late June)

Who knew there were some many Scandinavian people in Colorado? Well, you can come and meet a lot of them here. You can also try their food and drink, dress like Vikings and throw axes, or maybe even help raise the midsummer pole. Music and dancing, too. It's a smorgasbord of fun.

Independence Day Fireworks (July)

The town puts on a very nice fireworks display for America's birthday. The rockets rise over Lake Estes for 20-25 minutes. Time is sparse between all the kabooms, but you'll still have plenty of time to ooooo and ahhhhh to your heart's content!

Rooftop Rodeo (July)

Often called "The Rodeo with Altitude", this is one of Estes Park's signature events. Sanctioned by the PRCA and the WPRA, the Rooftop Rodeo is THE place to be for serious riders, ropers, and animals who compete at the highest levels.

Bring your hat, buckle, and boots for an exciting and great time.

Learn more at https://www.rooftoprodeo.com.

♥ Highly Recommended

Estes Park Wine Festival (August)

This is the second and largest wine event of the year, with many wineries, retail vendors, and food vendors filling in the space at Bond Park. Only adults and their designated drivers are allowed in, and there's no re-entry once you leave.

All wineries that participate must be licensed in Colorado, so this is the perfect event if you're interested in our local grapes.

Longs Peak Scottish-Irish Highland Festival (September)

When you start seeing more than a few people wearing kilts and other traditional clan uniforms around Estes Park, you know it must be time for the Longs Peak Scottish-Irish Highland Festival (aka "Scotfest").

Billed as the "Celtic Capital of North America," this year's event marks the 48th time for this three-day annual festival, which fills the Estes Park Fairgrounds.

Bagpipe competitions, highland dance, Scottish athletics (you gotta watch the caber toss), dog agility competitions, and premium Celtic music and food are ready for you and more than 100 Clans and Societies to enjoy.

Learn more at https://www.scotfest.com.

♥ Highly Recommended

Elk Fest (October)

The Town of Estes Park is already packed with elk watchers (and likely lots of elk) this time of the year, so why not hold another event in Bond Park? Yeah, it's busy for sure, but it's always fun.

Listen to locals and visitors compete for bragging rights in the elk bugling contests. Native American dancing, elk-inspired arts and crafts, food, drink, and more. Free to all.

Catch the Glow Christmas Parade & Celebration (Late November)

Just like many small-town parades from yesteryear. Dancers, marching bands, jugglers, and lots and lots of floats run right through downtown to the amazement of children and their parents who line the streets. Mr. and Mrs. Clause then hop off their float at Bond Park, where the children can visit them in the North Pole Workshop. Definitely a family-friendly event for all.

♥ Highly Recommended

Chapter 12

What Else Is There To Do?

Here are some other activities to consider, listed in alphabetical order.

Disc Golf

If you're into disc golf with some awesome scenery, you found your place. 18 holes. Tee times are suggested. $10 per person. You can pay at the pro shop just east of the Visitor Center at 690 Big Thompson.

Estes Park Museum

The history of Estes Park dates back to the mid-1800s, and this is the place to learn more about it. From Enos Mills and Isabella Byrd to Lord Dunraven and F.O. Stanley, and everyone in between. The museum is free and open to the public year-round.

During the summer months, the museum also offers two walking tours, which are led by local and very knowledgeable experts.

The first takes you on a trek through downtown where you'll learn about the early tenants and owners of many of these businesses, including the Stanley Bank, the movie theatre, and the original Estes Park Taffy Shop.

On the second tour, you'll visit the Birch Ruins, which overlooks the City Hall from high on the hill. Like the museum, these tours are free and open to the public.

Learn more at: https://estespark.colorado.gov/museum.

♥ Highly Recommended

Fishing

Lots of options for fishing around Estes Park: Inside RMNP, around Lake Estes (or below the dam), Mary's Lake, or anywhere along the rivers between here and Loveland or Longmont. A Colorado Fishing License is required.

Fly fishing for trout is the specialty, where the real "trick" is presenting the right fly at the right time at the right depth. This continues to mystify me, but I still love trying!

If you need some help with your gear or technique or strategies, you can always ask the person standing in the stream next to you. Or, you can get some hands-on professional instructions from the guides at **Kirks Fly Shop**, **Scot's Sporting Goods**, or **Flyfish Estes Park**.

♥ Highly recommended (all three).

BTW, if you want to get the little ones involved in fishing, the Trout Haven Fishing Pond might just fit the bill.

Golf

Choose between the 18-hole course or the 9-hole course. Both are city-owned and managed, and both are well-maintained. Use the *Estes Park Golf Courses* mobile app for tee times, tips, GPS-based range finding, and a digital scorecard.

♥ Highly Recommended

Note: Play can get complicated, especially in the fall when the big bull elk decide to corral their harems between you and the green. Please don't try to play through. Just give them a (very) wide berth and take the drop on the other side.

> There's nothing in the PGA
> Rulebook about elk.

Hiking

Entire books are filled with great information about all of the hiking trails in the area. So, we're not going to go into great detail here.

The following trails are mostly easy trails where you can take the kids or the grandparents, and walk at whatever pace you want.

If you want to investigate these options and others as well, you might appreciate the pocket-sized *Rocky Mountain Day Hikes* book. It's only $5 and covers 24 hikes of varying difficulty. You can grab your own copy at Safeway, Macdonald Books, and several other places in town.

Easy Trails

- Alluvial Fan

- Sprague Lake

- Bear Lake

- Lilly Lake

- Alberta Falls

- Adams Falls (on the Grand Lake side)

Medium

(longer and/or greater elevation changes)

- Lake Estes

- Nymph Lake, Dream Lake, and Emerald Lake (all on the same trail)

- Lake Haiyaha

- Mills Lake

Harder

(know before you go)

On one of our earliest trips here, we naively started up Longs Peak before driving back to the airport. Let's just say that it didn't take us long to know we weren't going to get very far, especially in the limited time we had and the fact that we were woefully unprepared. Lesson learned: Research the longer trails and plan accordingly

We don't try many of the difficult trails now. However, we still want to hike the leg of the Ute Pass Trail that starts up on Trail Ridge Road and ends in Beaver Meadows. Maybe this year ...

Live Music

Live music is alive and well in Estes Park. Bluegrass, Classic Rock, Jazz, Celtic, Open-mic nights, karaoke, and more. The list of local and regional bands and artists changes every weekend, but here are some local places where you can usually feel the beat and dance your feet.

- The Rock Inn

- The Barrel

- The Wheel Bar

- Full Throttle Distillery

- Bull Pin

- Cousin Pat's

- Snowy Peaks Winery

Cowboy Brad

If you've ever been to Estes Park, you've probably already heard of Cowboy Brad (aka Brad Fitch). If not, be sure to watch for him on your next visit.

A favorite of locals and guests alike, Brad brings the sounds of John Denver back to life with regular, free concerts and sing-alongs in Bond Park during the summer months.

Pretty sure we can say even the local animals like his Western music melodies. This was demonstrated in 2023, when an elk walked right up to him in Bond Park as he played. Brad just kept on singing while the audience stood in amazement.

♥ Highly Recommended

Mountain Coaster

Alpine mountain coasters are a lot of fun and the Mustang Mountain Coaster on Dry Gulch Road lives up to the hype. Age and weight limits apply.

Movies

Estes Park has two theaters: The Historic Park Theater downtown and the Real Mountain Theater across Highway 34 from the

Visitor Center. You can count on the Historic Park Theater for more documentaries and niche movies, while the Real Mountain Theatre has more of the current blockbusters.

RMNP Activities

Beyond the driving, hiking, and sightseeing, there's still a lot to do in RMNP, including Ranger-led walks and talks, horseback riding, fishing, bird watching, and more. Hey, maybe your youngsters want to be Junior Rangers!

There are RMNP Visitor Centers at both entrance gates in Estes Park, as well as a museum just before you get to Moraine Park.

Learn more about all of it at https://www.nps.gov/romo/planyourvisit/things2do.htm

Stargazing

Generally speaking, you need to get away from the city lights for the best views of our stars and planets. Viewing from a higher altitude provides generous benefits, too. In Estes Park, we're mostly shielded from the big city lights generated by Fort Collins, Denver, Boulder, and beyond. Our humidity is pretty low, too. Add in the altitude and you're in a really good spot to see a LOT of stars at night.

When Trail Ridge Road is open, we like to stretch out on our reclining folding chairs at the Forest Canyon Overlook. The Milky Way and its carpet of stars reach across the sky. Constellations and planets leap from the darkness.

Don't even get us started on the outstanding meteor showers. Beautiful! In 2020, we watched the Neowise comet from the trail north of Rock Cut (along with a hundred or so other friends). It was awesome!

By the way, Estes Park has its very own observatory! See https://www.angelsabove.org/ for more info.

The Stanley Hotel Tour(s)

They say Stephen King was inspired to write his best-seller, "The Shining" after a stay at the Stanley Hotel in 1974. But, we all still wonder whether the Stanley Hotel is really haunted or not.

Even if you aren't staying at The Stanley, you can still take the popular Stanley Hotel Tour and see if any apparitions speak to you along the way. Go ahead, be brave, and take the Night Tour if you think you're up for it.

Do you want to know even more about Stephen King's experience? In 2023, The Stanley Hotel debuted "The Shining Tour" and the new "Shining Suite", including the re-created bathroom scene and the infamous axe.

By the way, The Stanley Hotel also offers a variety of other events, entertainment, and activities across their large campus on the hill, including a resident magician show and Stanley Live – their relatively new event center.

Weddings

Not surprisingly, there are a lot of people who want to get married in RMNP. However, you do need a special permit, and you do need to plan ahead.

Warning: All of the approved wedding locations in the park are also open to the public, so you may end up with a few 'guests' photobombing your wedding pics.

The Town of Estes Park has a wide selection of supporting businesses for your nuptials as well, including wedding planners, reception events/locations, photographers, hair and makeup, catering, floral, and, let's not forget the oh-so-special honeymoon suite!

Chapter 13

Estes Park Essentials

Think of this as the reference section ... good info about things you may need to know about when visiting Estes Park.

Altitude Sickness

> *Note: The following is intended to be helpful information, and should not be considered as medical advice.*

The altitude in Estes Park is about 7,500 feet above sea level. At the Alpine Visitor Center (the peak of Trail Ridge Road), the altitude is 11,796 feet above sea level. Unless you live at a similar altitude, the chances of someone in your group experiencing altitude sickness are pretty good.

At higher altitudes, oxygen is less concentrated in the atmosphere. The higher you go, the less there is. This leads to lower levels of oxygen in your body tissues – a condition called hypoxia.

Altitude sickness (also referred to as Mountain Sickness or Acute Mountain Sickness) can occur when you gain altitude too quickly. For example, when flying here on a plane that originates in Houston, TX (altitude: 79 ft), or Ames, IA (altitude: 942 feet), or Los Angeles, CA (altitude: 305 feet).

Symptoms usually appear within 12-24 hours of arriving and can include dizziness, headaches, anxiety, nausea, and muscle aches. For many, these symptoms are manageable and will reduce as your body gets used to the new altitude. However, everyone reacts differently.

The most common advice to overcome these symptoms is to drink plenty of non-alcoholic liquids and just take it easy. If possible, go back to a lower altitude (e.g., Loveland, Longmont, Denver) so you can acclimate a little longer.

If your symptoms are severe – for example, if you have trouble walking, or experience a loss of coordination, severe headache, tightening of your chest, a cough that produces white or pink foam, etc. – seek medical attention immediately.

Seek medical attention immediately.

These may be symptoms of a serious, life-threatening condition, including pulmonary edema (fluid in the lungs) and/or cerebral edema (fluid in the brain).

Electric Vehicle (EV) Charging Stations

The Town of Estes Park has ChargePoint charging stations available to the public on a first-come-first-served basis at:

- The North side of the Town Hall Parking Lot at 335 E. Elkhorn Ave.

- The East side of the Town's parking structure at 691 N. Saint Vrain

- The Estes Park Visitor Center at 500 Big Thompson Ave.

You must use the ChargePoint mobile app to access and use these charging stations.

For additional info, please refer to https://estespark.colorado.gov/electricvehicles.

Additional EV charging may be available at the following locations.

- Additional ChargePoint stations can be found at the YMCA of the Rockies and on Tunnel Road just passed the YMCA of the Rockies

- Tesla Destination Chargers can be found at the Stanley Hotel, Sweet Basilico, River Stone Resorts, and Beaver Brook on the River.

- Several EV Connect charging stations can be found in the parking lot at The Country Market

- A Blink charging station is located at Twin Owls Restaurant.

Estes Valley Library

Most of us don't visit the library on our vacations, but if you're looking for some free Wi-Fi or need to catch up on your newspapers and magazines, this is the place. It's located just east of City Hall.

Fast Food Chains

We get it. Sometimes you just need something that you know. Options are fairly limited in Estes Park, but here they are (in alphabetical order):
- Dairy Queen
- Domino's Pizza
- Jimmy Johns
- McDonald's
- Starbucks (2)
- Subway (2)

Getting Here

By Airplane

There are no options for flying in or out of Estes Park (except for rescue/fire operations and Flight For Life®).

- Denver International Airport (DEN) is the closest major airport to Estes Park.

- Colorado Springs Airport (COS) is another option that comes with a 3+ hour drive time to get here after landing.

Estes Park Shuttle

If you're heading to Estes Park from Denver International Airport (or heading back to the airport), you may want to consider using the Estes Park Shuttle. This locally owned service has many options for one-way or roundtrips from Denver International Airport, Union Station (in Denver), Boulder, Longmont, and Loveland. For more info, please refer to their website at https://www.estesparkshuttle.com/.

♥ Highly Recommended

By Car/Truck/Motorcycle/RV

Highway 34 from Loveland/Fort Collins – Hwy 34 is a two-lane road with occasional passing lanes on the uphill side. Spectacular views in the canyon just west of Loveland. Keep your eyes open for Big Horn Sheep. If you're into fly fishing, watch the river for your fellow anglers.

Highway 36 (from Boulder) and Highway 66 (from Longmont) – These two major arteries merge in Lyons and account for the majority of traffic coming into Estes Park. Like Highway 34, this is a two-lane road with occasional passing lanes on the uphill side. This is always busy in the summer and fall, so plan on some delays.

Highway 7 – This is another option from Lyons. A bit off the beaten path, but the [incredibly] steep-walled canyons are a sight to behold. Between Allenspark and Estes Park, you'll drive past The Chapel on the Rock - one of our Must-See Destinations.

Trail Ridge Road (Highway 34) – If you're coming from the west there's only one option. Highway 34 (on the west side of RMNP) starts/ends in Granby. Take it north through Grand Lake and you'll soon enter Rocky Mountain National Park. This two-lane highway is the highest continuously paved road in the U.S. and offers endless, spectacular views at the higher elevations. Another Must-See Destination.

Word of caution, if you have a fear of heights, consider letting someone else drive.

Note: Trail Ridge Road is closed between late October/early November and Memorial Day due to snow at the higher elevations.

Gift Shops

There aren't any of the big box stores like Wal-Mart, Home Depot, or Target in Estes Park. But if you're looking for a gift shop, you won't be disappointed. They are everywhere!

Here are a few we like for their unique selections.

- Earthwood Artisans

- Macdonald's Bookstore

- Inkwell & Brew

- Christmas Shoppe

- Simply Christmas (Did I mention that Emma is a Christmas junkie?)

- Sticks and Stones

- Trendz

All of these are ♥ Highly Recommended

Grocery Stores

Safeway

The widest selection for groceries in Estes Park is the Safeway in Stanley Village. Granted it may not be as expansive as the grocery stores you might find in larger cities, but they do a great job with produce, meats, pre-made meals, the deli section, and paper/plasticware. Their bakery is wonderful! They also have a full-service pharmacy.

Country Market

The Country Market is much smaller but has a good selection of common staples, produce, and meat. They also have a terrific deli counter loaded with grab-and-go food, soups, and sandwiches.

If you're looking for some core fundamentals, consider the **Dollar Store or the Dollar Tree**. They have small, refrigerated/freezer sections, pantry items, and a lot of foil pans, paper plates, plasticware, etc.

Other smaller options for grocery shopping include **La Mexicana & Carniceria Mini Market**, **Famous Eastside Food Store**, and the **Estes Mini Mart**.

Healthcare

Emergency? Call 9-1-1

EMS/ambulance services are available, as well as access to Flight-for-Life.

Emergency Room and Urgent Care Services

Estes Park Health (Emergency Room/Hospital)

Open 24/7
(970) 586-2317
555 Prospect Ave

Estes Park Urgent Care

Hours: M-F 10a-6p; Sat/Sun 9a-7p
(970) 586-2317
420 Steamer Drive, Suite 101

Pharmacies

While speaking with the Safeway pharmacist a couple of years back, I was surprised to learn that quite a few visitors send their prescriptions to Estes Park to pick up while they're visiting. So, here you go.

We have two pharmacies in town, and they share the same parking lot.

Rocky Mountain Pharmacy

(970) 586-5577
www.rockymountainpharmacy.com
455 E Wonderview Ave B1, Estes Park, CO 80517

Safeway Pharmacy

(970) 577-8226
local.pharmacy.safeway.com
451 E Wonderview Ave, Estes Park, CO 80517

Eye Care/Glasses

Aspen Eyecare

Optometrist
(970) 586-4418
www.aspen-eyecare.com

Wendy's Optical

Optician
(970) 310-8344
343 S St Vrain Ave., Unit 7, Estes Park, CO 80517

Veterinarians

There are two veterinarians in town. We happen to use Animal Hospital of the Rockies when our puppy needs care, but our friends and neighbors speak highly of the Animal Medical Center, too.

Animal Medical Center-Estes Park

(970) 586-6898
www.amcestes.com

Animal Hospital of the Rockies

(970) 586-4703
www.estesparkpetvet.com

Liquor Stores

Grocery stores are allowed to sell beer and wine. But, if you're looking for liquor, you'll need to head to one of five liquor stores in town. By the way, liquor stores carry beer and wine, too!

Longhorn Liquor Mart and **Mountain Dew Liquor** are our favorites. In addition to having a good selection of products, they consistently have the lowest prices, too.

♥ Highly Recommended

Marijuana

While we're mentioning vices, marijuana use (in private) is legal for adults in Colorado. Estes Park does not have any licensed retail outlets for marijuana, though CBD-based products are plentiful. The closest retail locations for recreational and medicinal marijuana are in Lyons and Fort Collins.

Media

We have two newspapers and one TV channel. Several radio stations can be tuned in (depending on where you are), but there's only one FM radio station that is located in town - KREV-LP (104.7 FM).

The Estes Park Trail-Gazette

Originally a magazine for tourists, the original *Estes Park Trail* came to life in 1910. Currently, the *Estes Park Trail*-Gazette is published by Media News Group. Each weekly printed edition costs 75 cents and is published on Fridays.

The Estes Park News

The Estes Park News is a much thicker (and free) newspaper. Good content for visitors and locals alike. A new edition is published on Fridays.

The Rocky Mountain Channel

If you turn on any TV in Estes Park, you're sure to find and hear the voice of Nick Mollé as you're surfing through the channels. He's been exploring every corner of RMNP (and Estes Park) for more than 20 years.

Weather

With an average of 300 days of sunshine per year, you're almost guaranteed good weather during your visits, regardless of what time of year you join us.

Summers generally bring highs in the mid-80s with sporadic afternoon thunderstorms that roll through pretty fast. Those temps drop to the 40s or 50s at night.

We're on the east side of the Rockies, so we (usually) don't get too much snow in the winter. When there is snow, it often comes as light snow showers that bring 1-2 inches of snow. However, that melts pretty fast with all of our sunshine. Typical winter temps range from lows in the teens to highs in the 40s. Most of our snow comes in March.

Elevation Matters

When you're heading into RMNP, please consider your elevation. It may be a gorgeous 80-degree day in Estes Park. However, it might be snowing at the Alpine Visitor Center or anywhere in the higher elevations. Our best advice is to dress in multiple, light layers. This enables you to maintain your personal comfort level based on the number of layers you're wearing, regardless of the circumstances.

Our 300 days of sunshine *and* the altitude mean you should slather on the sunscreen when venturing outside. Hats are a great idea, too.

Chapter 14

Mobile Apps & Websites

Mobile Apps

Please visit the Apple App Store or Google Play to download the mobile apps mentioned below.

- NPS App (National Park Service) – One app, every park.

- Recreation.gov Mobile App

- National Park Trail Guide

- Park Mobile – Enables you to pay for parking. Great also for adding more time for parking.

- Estes Parking – See if there's space in key parking lots.

- Estes Park Golf Courses – Book a tee time, get tips, GPS-based range finding, and keep score on the embedded digital scorecard.

- Mapping/Traffic Apps – Google Maps, Apple Maps, Waze – They're all pretty good, so pick your fave.

Websites

Rocky Mountain National Park (NPS):
https://www.nps.gov/romo/index.htm

RMNP Web Cams (including the entrance gates):
https://www.nps.gov/romo/learn/photosmultimedia/webcams.
htm

NPS Species List for RMNP:
https://irma.nps.gov/NPSpecies/Search/SpeciesList/ROMO.

Recreation.gov

- Purchase Timed Entry Passes:
  https://www.recreation.gov/timed-entry/10086910

- Purchase Hiker Shuttle Reservations:
  https://www.recreation.gov/timed-entry/10088647/tick
  et/10088648

Estes Park Museum: https://estespark.colorado.gov/museum

Estes Park Event Center:
https://www.estesparkeventscomplex.com

The Official Tourism Website for Estes Park:
https://www.visitestespark.com/

Facebook

Official NPS RMNP Facebook page:
https://www.facebook.com/RockyNPS
♥ Highly recommended

Elk In Estes (Private):
https://www.facebook.com/groups/1953590664961519/
♥ Highly recommended

Everything Estes Park (Private):
https://www.facebook.com/groups/EverythingEstesPark

Estes Valley Area Road Reports (Private):
https://www.facebook.com/groups/EstesValleyRoadReports/

Chapter 15

Back Matter

About Us

The *Insider Guide to Estes Park and Rocky Mountain National Park* is written and produced by a husband-and-wife team who live and breathe in Estes Park all year long.

We fell in love with Estes Park and RMNP on our first visit in 1994. We came. We saw. We were astounded. Following that trip, we returned every year – sometimes two or three times per year. Every single time we visited, we left with the same goal in mind.

We need to move here ... and
soon!

It took us a long time, but on the 25th anniversary of our very first trip, we finally did it. We moved to our favorite vacation spot - a seemingly lifelong dream come true. Estes Park is now our home and we have no intention of ever leaving.

Why We Wrote This Book

Over the last 30 years, we've stayed in dozens of hotels, cabins, rental homes, and campsites. We've hiked the trails. We've eaten at most of the restaurants and shopped at many of the stores. We've asked, "Where are those elk today?" hundreds of times. And, we've scrimped and saved so we could stay longer and come back sooner.

Over those many years, we learned a few tricks and techniques to maximize our experience in RMNP and Estes Park.

We get you.

We understand what you're going through to get here, and we want to help you. That's how this book came about.

This is not the official visitor's guide.

The official visitor's guide and many of the other publications tell you about **everything**. And that's one of the things that makes this book different (and, we think, better).

We don't tell you about
everything because everything
is too much.

There are hundreds, if not thousands of possible decisions you need to make regarding where you're staying, where you're eating, what to do, when to come, what to buy, and how to do it all. Sigh ... **TL; DR** (Too Long; Didn't Read).

We narrow all of that down for you by providing specific recommendations that can help you make the most of your time in Estes Park and RMNP. Easy to find. Quick reads. From someone just like you.

We give you honest and unbiased advice.

Please Tell Your Friends

If you enjoyed what we shared with you, we'd greatly appreciate it if you'd tell your friends about it.

The Companion Website: EstesParkInsider.com

estesparkinsider.com

Depending on the date you purchased it, we might still be working on updates to the website. (Thank you for your patience.)

Once it's done, we'll be adding even more content that we think will help make your next trip to Estes Park and RMNP an even better experience. Some of our planned enhancements include:

- Timely and up-to-date content about road repairs and

construction, as well as the status of construction for the new Fall River Entrance and the Moraine Park Campground.

- Info about any changes to the Timed Entry Reservation processes.

- Updates to our dining recommendations, including any new restaurants we've tried and liked, as well as any dining options that have improved since we wrote this.

- A photo gallery of the amazing things you'll see while you're here.

- Corrections to any typos we may have missed while preparing this edition, or if we were incorrect about something.

Made in the USA
Las Vegas, NV
01 August 2024

93224902R00075